Animals in the
Forest

By John Wood

KidHaven
PUBLISHING

Published in 2018 by
KidHaven Publishing, an Imprint of Greenhaven Publishing, LLC
353 3rd Avenue
Suite 255
New York, NY 10010

Designer: Matt Rumbelow
Editor: Holly Duhig

Cataloging-in-Publication Data

Names: Wood, John.
Title: Animals in the forest / John Wood.
Description: New York : KidHaven Publishing, 2018. | Series: Where animals live | Includes index.
Identifiers: ISBN 9781534523685 (pbk.) | 9781534523661 (library bound) | ISBN 9781534525122 (6 pack) | ISBN 9781534523678 (ebook)
Subjects: LCSH: Forest animals–Juvenile literature.
Classification: LCC QL112.W66 2018 | DDC 591.73–dc23

Printed in the United States of America

3 5944 00140 0769

CPSIA compliance information: Batch #CW18KL: For further information contact Greenhaven Publishing LLC, New York, New York at 1-844-317-7404.

Please visit our website, www.greenhavenpublishing.com. For a free color catalog of all our high-quality books, call toll free 1-844-317-7404 or fax 1-844-317-7405.

Photo credits: Abbreviations: l-left, r-right, b-bottom, t-top, c-center, m-middle.
Covertr - Markuso; Covertm - Michael Kuijl; Covertl - geertweggen; Coverbl - Martin Mecnarowski; Coverbr - Geoffrey Kuchera. 2 - PlusONE. 3: bg - karen roach; br - geertweggen. 4 - FloridaStock. 5: bg - karen roach; tl - bikeriderlondon; tr - Ehrman Photographic; m - Banana Republic images; bl - Joe Belanger; br - GUDKOV ANDREY. 6 - Africa Studio. 7 - Vadim Georgiev. 8: t - Maria Jeffs; b - Rudmer Zwerver. 9 - David Maska. 10 - Geoffrey Kuchera. 11 - Miroslav Hlavko. 12 - Michael Kuijl. 13 - Dieter Hawlan. 14 - Martin Mecnarowski. 15 - Ondrej Prosicky. 16 - duangnapa_b. 17 - CyberKat. 18 - geertweggen. 19 - Spreewald-Birgit. 20 - wandee007. 21 - Rich Carey. 22 - Konstantin Tronin. 23 - Karel Gallas. Images are courtesy of Shutterstock.com, with thanks to Getty Images, Thinkstock Photo, and iStockphoto.

CONTENTS

Page 4   What Is a Habitat?

Page 6   What Is a Forest?

Page 8   Types of Forest Habitats

Page 10   Foxes

Page 12   Bears

Page 14   Woodpeckers

Page 16   Bats

Page 18   Squirrels

Page 20   Forests in Danger

Page 22   Endangered Animals

Page 24   Glossary and Index

Words that look like this can be found in the glossary on page 24.

WHAT IS A
HABITAT?

A habitat is a place where an animal lives. It provides the animal with food, shelter, and everything else it needs to survive.

Shown here is a woodpecker living in a tree.

There are different habitats around the world. Each one is home to many different animals.

forests

grasslands

deserts

oceans

jungles

WHAT IS A FOREST?

A forest is a type of habitat that is covered in plants and trees. Forests are often found in places that experience all four seasons.

[summer] [autumn] [winter] [spring]

6

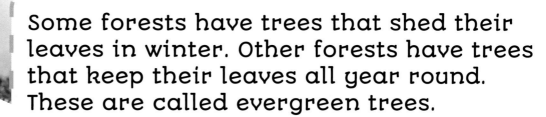

Some forests have trees that shed their leaves in winter. Other forests have trees that keep their leaves all year round. These are called evergreen trees.

evergreen trees

TYPES OF
FOREST HABITATS

Forests are home to many different animal habitats. The trees in forests provide homes for many animals. Some animals also live on the forest floor.

8

Forests in places with many hills might also have caves. Caves provide animals with shelter and make great animal homes.

FOXES

Foxes make burrows in the forest floor. A fox's burrow is called a den. Foxes sleep and look after their young in their dens.

A young fox is sometimes called a kit.

Foxes like to make their dens in dry soil. The entrance to a fox's den is very small; however, as it goes deeper, the den becomes wider.

kits in a den

BEARS

Bears make the whole forest their home. From towering trees to forest streams, there are no parts of the forest that bears will not explore!

Bears make dens underground or use caves as their homes. They sleep in their homes during the cold winter months. This state is called torpor.

WOODPECKERS

Woodpeckers get their name from the way they peck at the side of trees with their long beaks. They do this to find insects to eat.

Woodpeckers also make their homes by pecking holes into trees. These holes are called woodpecker nests.

Woodpeckers can peck 20 times per second!

15

BATS

Bats' homes are called roosts. Bats make their roosts in all sorts of places, especially in caves and trees. When bats settle in their roosts, it is called roosting.

Bats sleep upside down in their roosts.

When female bats have babies, they roost in warmer places such as tree hollows. In this hollow, the bat and her baby are sheltered from the wind.

a bat in a tree hollow

SQUIRRELS

Squirrels also make their homes in trees. During the winter, they make dens in tree hollows. They fill these with moss and leaves for extra warmth.

In warmer weather, squirrels make nests called dreys. They are made out of twigs, grass, and dry leaves. They make dreys in the branches of trees.

a squirrel in its drey

DANGER

People cut down the trees in forests and use the wood to make things such as paper, furniture, and even houses. When many trees in a forest get cut down, it is called deforestation.

deforestation

Deforestation makes animal habitats smaller and destroys many animal homes. Without their homes, it is hard for these animals to survive. When animals find it hard to survive, they are said to be endangered.

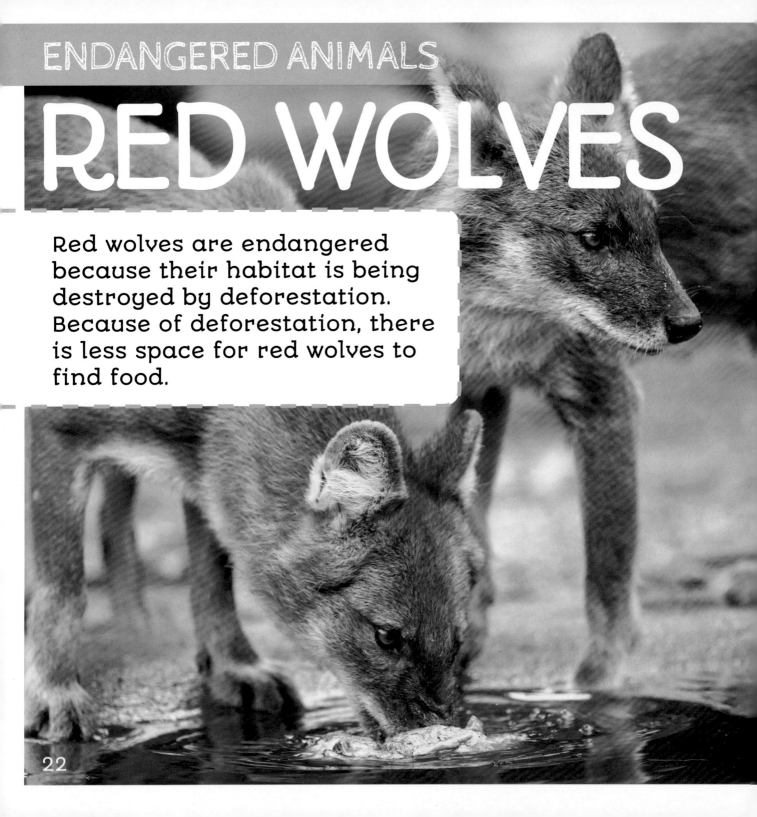

RED WOLVES

Red wolves are endangered because their habitat is being destroyed by deforestation. Because of deforestation, there is less space for red wolves to find food.

RED PANDAS

Red pandas make their homes high up in trees. They are also endangered because people are cutting down their homes.

GLOSSARY

beak	the hard, pointed mouth of a bird
burrow	a hole or tunnel dug by an animal
endangered	in danger of dying out
hollow	a small hole or groove, usually in trees
moss	a small, green plant that grows in damp habitats
shelter	protection from danger and harsh weather
soil	the upper layer of earth in which plants grow

Index

caves 9, 13, 16

deforestation 20–22

den 10–11, 13, 18

dreys 19

endangered 21–23

evergreens 7

habitat 4–6, 8, 21–22

hollow 17–18

insect 14

leaves 7, 18–19

nest 15, 19

roost 16–17

shelter 4, 9, 17

soil 11

streams 12

torpor 13